P9-CPW-431

Nita Mehta's

Zer Oil
Cooking

Nita Mehta

B.Sc. (Home Science), M.Sc. (Food and Nutrition), Gold Medalist

SNAB

Nita Mehta's

Zero Oil cooking

© Copyright 2007 **SNAB** **Publishers Pvt Ltd**

WORLD RIGHTS RESERVED: The contents - all recipes, photographs and drawings are original and copyrighted. No portion of this book shall be reproduced, stored in a retrieval system or transmitted by any means, electronic, mechanical, photocopying, recording or otherwise, without the written permission of the publishers.

While every precaution is taken in the preparation of this book, the publishers and the author assume no responsibility for errors or omissions. Neither is any liability assumed for damages resulting from the use of information contained herein.

TRADEMARKS ACKNOWLEDGED: Trademarks used, if any, are acknowledged as trademarks of their respective owners. These are used as reference only and no trademark infringement is intended upon.

ISBN 81-7869-163-9

Exclusive Distributor:

**PRODUCTIONS**
DIVISION OF: INFORMATION SCIENCE INDUSTRIES (CANADA) LIMITED

1169 Parisien St., Ottawa, Ont., K1B 4W4,
Tel: 613.745.3098 Fax: 613.745.7533
e-mail: amproductions@rogers.com
web: www.amproductions.ca

Published by:

SNAB
Publishers Pvt. Ltd.
3A/3 Asaf Ali Road,
New Delhi - 110002
Tel: 23252948, 23250091
Telefax:91-11-23250091
INDIA

Editorial and Marketing office:
E-159, Greater Kailash-II, N.Delhi-48
Fax: 91-11-29225218, 29229558
Tel: 91-11-29214011, 29218727, 29218574
E-Mail: nitamehta@email.com, nitamehta@nitamehta.com
*Website:*http://www.nitamehta.com
Website: http://www.snabindia.com

Printed at:
PRESSTECH LITHO PVT LTD, NEW DELHI

Price: $ 5.95

Contents

snacks   6

salads and soups   14

vegetables   19

chicken   28

fish   35

desserts   41

Introduction

Watch your weight, the delicious way!

Watch your weight the delicious way!

Zero oil does not mean the end of culinary pleasures. In fact without an oil barriers your taste buds will begin to appreciate many taste-shades and flavour-nuances that you never experienced before.

These Zero Oil recipes include the right quality and quantity of proteins, carbohydrates, vitamins and minerals without adding to the calorie count. There is no need to skip a meal if you use these recipes.

I believe that this book will help those people who have a heart problem or a weight problem. The food in this book will open up a new world of joyful and delicious meals for them. They can eat without stress, knowing that they are eating Zero Oil!

Nita Mehta

INTERNATIONAL CONVERSION GUIDE

These are not exact equivalents; they've been rounded-off to make measuring easier.

WEIGHTS & MEASURES

METRIC	IMPERIAL
15 g	½ oz
30 g	1 oz
60 g	2 oz
90 g	3 oz
125 g	4 oz (¼ lb)
155 g	5 oz
185 g	6 oz
220 g	7 oz
250 g	8 oz (½ lb)
280 g	9 oz
315 g	10 oz
345 g	11 oz
375 g	12 oz (¾ lb)
410 g	13 oz
440 g	14 oz
470 g	15 oz
500 g	16 oz (1 lb)
750 g	24 oz (1½ lb)
1 kg	30 oz (2 lb)

LIQUID MEASURES

METRIC	IMPERIAL
30 ml	1 fluid oz
60 ml	2 fluid oz
100 ml	3 fluid oz
125 ml	4 fluid oz
150 ml	5 fluid oz (¼ pint/1 gill)
190 ml	6 fluid oz
250 ml	8 fluid oz
300 ml	10 fluid oz (½ pint)
500 ml	16 fluid oz
600 ml	20 fluid oz (1 pint)
1000 ml	1¾ pints

CUPS & SPOON MEASURES

METRIC	IMPERIAL
1 ml	¼ tsp
2 ml	½ tsp
5 ml	1 tsp
15 ml	1 tbsp
60 ml	¼ cup
125 ml	½ cup
250 ml	1 cup

HELPFUL MEASURES

METRIC	IMPERIAL
3 mm	1/8 in
6 mm	¼ in
1 cm	½ in
2 cm	¾ in
2.5 cm	1 in
5 cm	2 in
6 cm	2½ in
8 cm	3 in
10 cm	4 in
13 cm	5 in
15 cm	6 in
18 cm	7 in
20 cm	8 in
23 cm	9 in
25 cm	10 in
28 cm	11 in
30 cm	12 in (1ft)

HOW TO MEASURE

When using the graduated metric measuring cups, it is important to shake the dry ingredients loosely into the required cup. Do not tap the cup on the table, or pack the ingredients into the cup unless otherwise directed. Level top of cup with a knife. When using graduated metric measuring spoons, level top of spoon with a knife. When measuring liquids in the jug, place jug on a flat surface, check for accuracy at eye level.

OVEN TEMPERATURE

These oven temperatures are only a guide. Always check the manufacturer's manual.

	°C (Celsius)	°F (Fahrenheit)	Gas Mark
Very low	120	250	1
Low	150	300	2
Moderately low	160	325	3
Moderate	180	350	4
Moderately high	190	375	5
High	200	400	6
Very high	230	450	7

SNACKS

Chicken Pick-ups

Sauté marinated chicken and vegetables – present them on toothpicks for easy pick up!

Serves 10-12

INGREDIENTS

12 bite size boneless chicken (½" cubes)
2 tbsp cornstarch
½ egg, ½ tsp salt
1 onion - cut into 1" pieces and
separated (12 pieces)
1 green bell pepper - cut into ¾" squares
pieces (12 pieces)
4 tbsp stir fry sauce
1 tsp sesame seeds (*til*)
a few tooth picks

MARINADE (MIX TOGETHER)
½ tsp salt
¾ tsp white pepper, or to taste
1 tsp garlic paste (2-3 flakes of garlic-
crushed to a paste)
½ tsp red chilli flakes
3-4 tbsp tomato sauce
1 tsp soya sauce
2 tsp red chilli sauce

METHOD

1   Mix chicken with cornstarch, egg and salt. Boil 5-6 cups water. Add chicken to boiling water and cook for 2-3 minutes or till cooked. Remove chicken with a strainer. Keep aside.

2   Marinate the chicken cubes, onion and the green peppers in the marinade mixture. Keep aside till serving time.

3   Heat a non stick pan/skillet. Reduce heat. Add the marinated chicken and vegetables and saute for 2-3 minutes, keeping them in a single layer in the pan.

4   Add stir fry sauce. Sprinkle some sesame seeds. Check seasonings.

5   Skewer an onion piece, then a chicken cube and lastly a green pepper piece on the tooth pick. Serve hot.

Baked Garbanzo Rounds

Taste the yogurt and mint in these golden rounds.

Makes 12

INGREDIENTS

1½ cups baked garbanzo beans (*kabuli channa*) - boiled or 2½ cups canned garbanzo beans/chickpeas
1 tsp ginger -garlic paste
4 tbsp chopped coriander/cilantro leaves
1 tsp salt, or to taste, ½ tsp oregano
some black pepper to taste
1 green chilli - very finely chopped
8 tbsp yogurt
1 tbsp dry mint (dry *poodina*)
1 cup dry bread crumbs, approx.

METHOD

1 Mash cooked garbanzo beans/chickpeas with a potato masher to a smooth paste. Add ginger-garlic paste, chopped chilli, coriander, salt, oregano and pepper. Add about 4 tbsp yogurt, just enough to bind the mixture into balls. Mix lightly with the hands.

2 Divide the mixture into 12 equal balls. Press to form a flat round cutlet.

3 Mix the remaining 4 tbsp yogurt with mint and spread this over the cutlets on both sides. Roll cutlets in bread crumbs to coat all the sides.

4 Place on a greased baking tray or a rack covered with foil. Bake at 180°C/350°F for 25-30 minutes or until done. Serve garnished with green pepper strips (optional).

Sesame Potato Fingers

Enjoy the flavour of onions, chillies and sesame seeds – there's nothing missing except the oil!

Serves 6

INGREDIENTS

4 slices of brown bread
1 tsp white or black sesame seeds

POTATO PASTE
2 boiled potatoes - grated (1 cup)
2 tsp tomato sauce
¼ cup finely chopped onion
½ tomato - deseeded and very finely
chopped (¼ cup)
1 green chilli - deseeded and finely
chopped
3 tbsp chopped fresh coriander/cilantro
¾ tsp salt, ¼ tsp pepper
½ tsp lemon juice, or to taste

METHOD

1 Mix all the ingredients for the potato paste together in a bowl. Divide into 4 portions.

2 Spread each portion of the potato mixture on one slice of bread. Repeat with the remaining bread slices and potato portions.

3 Sprinkle some sesame seeds. Grill in an oven till the bread turns crisp.

4 Cut each slice into 3 long fingers and serve hot.

Baycorn Crostini

A richly-flavoured topping, crusty fresh bread covered with a tasty tomato spread – so who needs butter!

Serves 10-12

INGREDIENTS

1 French Loaf or garlic bread - cut into ¼"
thick diagonal slices
2 tbsp chopped parsley

BABY CORN TOPPING
150 g/4 oz baby corns - sliced into rounds
(1½ cups)
2 tsp vinegar
2 tsp soya sauce
1 tsp red chilli sauce
2 tbsp cornstarch dissolved in ½ cup water
½ tsp salt, ½ tsp pepper

TOMATO SPREAD
6-8 flakes garlic - crushed (1½ tsp)
¼ tsp red chilli powder
½ cup ready-made tomato puree
2 tbsp tomato sauce
1 tsp oregano, dried
½ tsp salt and ½ tsp pepper to taste

METHOD

1 To prepare the tomato spread, mix all the ingredients and cook on low heat for about 5 minutes, till thick. Keep aside.

2 To prepare the topping, mix all ingredients, except the baby corns in a heavy bottomed pan and then add the sliced baby corns. Keep on heat and cook on low heat, stirring continuously till the sauce coats the baby corns and they get cooked a little.

3 Spread some tomato spread on the bread slices (crostini). Arrange some baby corns in sauce on it. Press.

4 Sprinkle some parsley.

5 To serve, place crostini on a grill rack. Bake at 200°C/400°F for 7-8 minutes till a little crisp. Do not over cook otherwise they turn too hard.

Note: *If baby corns are not available, cooked or tinned corn may be substituted.*

Patrani Machhi

A mouth-watering mix of coconut, coriander, garlic and lemon seep into the fish. These Indian-style banana-leaf packets are microwaved.

Serves 4

INGREDIENTS

250 g/8 oz boneless fish, preferably Sole - cut into 1½" square pieces of ½" thickness
2 tbsp lemon juice, ¼ tsp salt
a banana leaf - cut into 5" squares
a few tooth picks

GREEN PASTE
4" piece of coconut (¼ of a coconut) - chopped
½ cup chopped coriander/cilantro
2 flakes garlic - chopped (½ tsp)
1 tbsp lemon juice
¼ tsp sugar, ½ tsp salt
2-3 tbsp water to grind

METHOD

1 Wash the fish. Put lemon and salt and leave for 15-20 minutes.

2 Wash the fish again and pat dry on a kitchen towel.

3 Grind the ingredients of the green paste coarsely in a mixer.

4 Smear each piece of fish with paste on both sides. Marinate for 1 hour or till serving time.

5 To serve, wrap each piece in a banana leaf square and secure with a tooth pick. Microwave for 3½ minutes. Give standing time for 1 minute. Serve wrapped in the leaf.

Chicken Club Sandwiches

A traditional club sandwich with all the trimmings – just replace the mayonnaise with creamy yogurt flavoured with minced onions and mustard.

Serves 4

2 Keep the shredded chicken and the chopped onion in a bowl and add enough whipped yogurt to get a paste, thick enough for the filling.

3 Season the filling by adding a dash of pepper, salt, mustard and chilli-garlic tomato sauce. Keep the seasonings of the filling a little strong because it may taste bland when spread on the bread.

4 Spread some mixture on a toasted bread slice. Keep a lettuce leaf on top. Arrange some tomato slices on top and sprinkle some salt and pepper on them.

5 Cover with another slice. Place egg slices and sprinkle some salt & pepper on them. Place another lettuce leaf and then arrange cucumber slices on the leaf.

6 Place another slice on it. Press well. Cut into 4 small triangles. Secure each sandwich with a toothpick.

7 Repeat with the other 3 slices to make another sandwich. Cut it also in the same way. Serve.

INGREDIENTS

1 chicken breast (125 g/4 oz)
½ tsp salt, 2 tbsp water
¾ cup yogurt - hang for 30 minutes in a cheese cloth and whipped till smooth
¼ cup finely chopped onion
1 tsp mustard
1 tsp chilli-garlic tomato sauce
salt and pepper to taste
6 bread slices, preferably brown - toasted
4 lettuce leaves
a few cucumber and tomato slices
2 hard-boiled eggs - cut into slices

METHOD

1 Microwave chicken with salt and water in a bowl covered with a cling wrap for 3 minutes. Cool and shred chicken into very small pieces. Keep aside.

Barbecued Chicken Drumsticks

Try these great-tasting drumsticks marinated for maximum flavour then baked.

Serves 4-6

INGREDIENTS

8-10 chicken drumsticks (legs)
1 onion - grated (½ cup)
salt and chilli flakes, to taste
2 tbsp vinegar
8 tbsp tomato puree
3-4 tbsp tomato ketchup
2 tsp Worcestershire sauce
1 tsp oregano
some onion rings & coriander/cilantro
to garnish

METHOD

1   Wash and pat dry the chicken.

2   Mix grated onion, vinegar, puree, sauces, salt, chilli flakes & oregano to prepare the marinade. Marinate the chicken pieces in this marinade for at least 3-4 hours.

3   Heat oven at 180˚C/350°F. Place chicken on a baking tray and cook for 20 minutes. Baste chicken pieces with the left over marinade. Bake again for 10 minutes.

4   Cook till the chicken is tender. Serve with onion rings, garnished with parsley or mint.

SALADS & SOUPS

Spinach & Mushroom Soup

A hearty, healthy milk-based soup – the pretty pale green colour increases eye appeal.

Serves 3-4

INGREDIENTS

1 cup roughly chopped spinach
1 cup very thinly sliced mushrooms
2 cups milk
1 flake garlic - crushed (½ tsp)
2 cups water mixed with 2 tbsp
cornstarch
4-6 peppercorns - crushed
1 tsp salt, or to taste
1 tsp lemon juice

METHOD

1 Boil chopped spinach with milk. Cook uncovered, for about 5 minutes or till spinach softens. Remove from heat. Cool. Strain the spinach and reserve the milk.

2 Put spinach in a blender with a little milk and roughly blend. Do not blend too much. Keep spinach puree aside.

3 Heat a pan, add garlic and mushrooms and saute for 3-4 minutes. Add the spinach puree and the reserved milk.

4 Add 2 cups water mixed with 2 tbsp cornstarch. Stir till it boils. Cook stirring frequently for 3-4 minutes. Add salt and freshly crushed pepper.

5 Remove from heat. Add lemon juice to taste. Serve hot

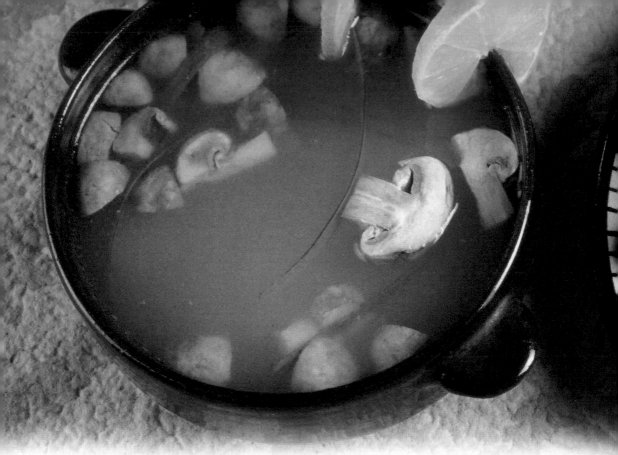

Clear Chicken & Mushroom Soup

It's clear and light – but the taste of lemon grass and ginger is smooth and bright!

Serves 4-5

INGREDIENTS

200 g/3 oz boneless chicken - cut into
1" pieces
6 cups water
1 stalk of lemon grass - chopped
1" piece ginger - chopped
120 g/4 oz mushrooms - cut into paper
thin slices
2-3 green chillies - slit long with seeds
removed
1 tsp salt, pepper to taste
2 tsp lemon juice (adjust to taste)

METHOD

1 Boil 6 cups water. Add the chicken, lemon grass and ginger and cook for 3 minutes or till cooked. Take out the chicken from stock. Let the stock simmer covered on low heat for 5 minutes. Discard lemon grass and ginger.

2 Shred chicken very finely as it is a clear soup and the chicken will sink if the pieces are even slightly big.

3 Keep stock back on heat. Add sliced mushrooms, shredded chicken, salt, pepper, green chillies and lemon juice. Give 2-3 boils. Serve hot, garnished with chopped fresh coriander/cilantro.

Microwaved Cauliflower Soup

An Indian-style soup of vegetables simmered in stock & milk, thickened with gram flour.

Serves 3-4

INGREDIENTS

1½ cups small florets of cauliflower
½ red or green bell pepper - cut into thin
strips (½ cup)
1 onion - finely chopped (½ cup)
a pinch of red chilli powder or to taste
1 tsp curry powder
1 soup/stock cube, 2 cups water
1 cup milk, 2 tbsp gram flour (*besan*)
2 tbsp chopped fresh coriander/cilantro
2 tbsp grated paneer

METHOD

1. Put cauliflower, bell pepper & onion in a large microwave-safe deep dish. Mix. Microwave for 8-10 minutes.

2. Add chilli powder, curry powder, soup cube and water. Mix well. Microwave for 4 minutes.

3. Meanwhile, add a little of the milk to the gram flour to make a paste. Gradually stir in the remaining milk, then stir the gram flour mixture and coriander into the soup. Mix. Cover & microwave for 6 minutes. Serve hot garnished with grated paneer.

Warm Stir Fried Salad

Warm salads are becoming increasingly popular – here is a nutritious mix of lean chicken cooked in its marinade and tossed with cabbage and carrots.

Serves 3-4

INGREDIENTS

125 g/4 oz boneless chicken breast - cut into thin strips
¾ cup shredded cabbage
½ red and ½ yellow pepper - thinly sliced
1 cup juliennes of carrot
½ tsp salt, ½ tsp pepper
2-3 tsp lemon juice
some lettuce leaves to serve

MARINADE

1 tsp soya sauce
½ tsp salt, ½ tsp pepper
1 tsp honey
½" piece ginger - cut into juliennes
1 tsp balsamic vinegar
1 tsp roasted white sesame seeds

METHOD

1. Marinate chicken strips with the ingredients given under marinade for 2-3 hours.

2. Cook chicken along with the marinade together for 2-3 minutes in a non stick pan till chicken is tender.

3. Add cabbage, carrot & bell peppers. Add ½ tsp each of salt and pepper.

4. Add 2-3 tsp lemon juice. Stir till just cooked but crunchy. Serve warm garnished with lettuce leaves.

VEGETABLES

Tikka Vegetables

When vegetables are treated with two marinades they absorb a lot of flavour – skewer them neatly and grill – voila!

Serves 6-8

INGREDIENTS

250 g/8 oz broccoli - cut into medium florets
250 g/8 oz cauliflower - cut into medium florets
8 mushrooms, 8 baby corns
1 tsp salt, 1 tsp lemon juice
1 tsp sugar
2 round slices of pineapple - cut into 1" triangles (8 pieces)
1 tomato - deseeded and cut into triangles
a few bamboo skewers

1ST MARINADE
1 tbsp lemon juice
¾ tsp carom seeds (*ajwain*) or oregano
½ tsp salt

2ND MARINADE
1½ cups thick yogurt - hang for 30 minutes in a cheese cloth
1 tbsp cornstarch
1 tbsp ginger- garlic paste
½ tsp salt, ¼ tsp pepper, lemon juice
¼ tsp kala namak, ¼ tsp salt

METHOD

1. Boil 6 cups of water in a large pan. Add 1 tsp salt, 1 tsp sugar and 1 tsp lemon juice. Add broccoli, cauliflower, mushrooms and baby corns to water. As soon as the boil returns after a minute, remove from heat. Drain. Wipe the pieces on a kitchen towel.

2. Spread the broccoli, cauliflower, mushrooms and baby corns on a tray and sprinkle the ingredients of the 1st marinade. Marinate the vegetables for 15 minutes.

3. Drain the vegetables of any excess juice.

4. Mix all the ingredients of the 2nd marinade in a large pan/bowl. Add the broccoli, cauliflower, mushrooms and baby corns to it and mix well.

5. Cover the grill rack of the oven with foil. Skewer the marinated broccoli, cauliflower, mushrooms & baby corns on bamboo skewers. Arrange pineapple pieces and tomatoes in between. Place on the foil and grill/broil for 15 minutes or till they turn brownish. Do not over cook as they turn dry. Serve hot.

Thai Red Curry

Assorted vegetables are simmered in this spicy red curry – none of the original ingredients are omitted except oil! I think it tastes better this way. Enjoy with steamed rice.

Serves 4-6

INGREDIENTS

RED CURRY PASTE
4-5 dry red chillies - soaked in ½ cup warm water for 10 minutes
½ cup chopped onion
1 tbsp minced or chopped garlic
½" piece galangal or ginger - sliced
1 stalk lemon grass or rind of 1 lemon
6 peppercorns (*saboot kali mirch*)
1 tsp salt, 1 tbsp lemon juice
1½ tsp coriander seeds (*dhania saboot*) and 1 tsp cumin (*jeera*) - roasted

VEGETABLES
6 baby corns - slit lengthwise
1 long thin brinjal - cut into ½" slices
5-6 florets of broccoli
2-3 mushrooms - sliced
¼ cup chopped bamboo shoots (optional)
3-4 green beans - cut into 2" lengths

OTHER INGREDIENTS
3 cups thin coconut milk
½ tsp soya sauce
15 basil leaves - chopped
salt to taste, ½ tsp brown sugar

METHOD

1 Dry roast cumin and coriander on a griddle/pan till fragrant.

2 Grind coriander and cumin with all the other ingredients of the red curry paste along with the water in which the chillies were soaked, to a very smooth paste.

3 Add the red curry paste in a deep pan and stir for a few seconds on low heat.

4 Add 3-4 tbsp of coconut milk. Add vegetables & cook for 2-3 minutes.

5 Add the rest of the coconut milk and soya sauce.

6 Simmer on low heat for 5-7 minutes till the vegetables are tender.

7 Add chopped basil leaves, salt and sugar to taste. Boil for 1 to 2 minutes. Serve hot with steamed rice or noodles.

Green Pea Masala

In Indian cooking spices & other ingredients can be gently heated on a hot skillet to release the essential flavour – good use is made of this technique in this cumin-flavoured vegetable medley.

Serves 4

INGREDIENTS

2 cups shelled peas - boiled or frozen
1 tsp cumin seeds (*jeera*)
3 onions - cut into rings (1½ cups)
½" piece ginger - finely chopped
¾ tsp garam masala
½ tsp red chilli powder
1 tsp ground coriander (*dhania powder*)
¼ cup ready-made tomato puree
2 tomatoes - chopped finely
1 green chilli - deseeded & slit
lengthwise, optional
¾ tsp salt or to taste
2 tbsp fresh coriander/cilantro - chopped
1 tsp lemon juice

METHOD

1. Heat a non stick pan, add cumin. Let it turn golden .

2. Add onion rings and stir till golden.

3. Add ginger and saute over medium heat for ½ minute.

4. Add tomato puree, garam masala, red chilli powder and ground coriander. Saute for 3-4 minutes till puree turns dry.

5. Add the boiled green peas and mix well. Add salt. Saute for 5 minutes.

6. Add chopped tomatoes and green chillies. Add green coriander/ cilantro. Stir fry for 3-4 minutes. Add lemon juice to taste. Sprinkle with garam masala and serve with hot chappatis.

Dill Potatoes

Boiled potatoes are wrapped in a creamy blend of yogurt and white sauce, flavoured with garlic and fresh dill.

Serves 4

INGREDIENTS

500 g/8 oz potatoes
1 tbsp lemon juice
4 flakes garlic - chopped (1 tsp)
1 tbsp plain flour (*maida*)
1½ cups milk
4 tbsp yogurt
1 tsp cornstarch
½ cup fresh dill (green soye leaves) -
finely chopped
2 green chillies - finely chopped, optional
½ tsp salt, ¼ tsp pepper, or to taste
a few drops of lemon juice

METHOD

1 Peel the potatoes. Cut them in ¼" thick, round slices.

2 Boil 4-5 cups of water with ½ tsp salt and 1 tbsp lemon juice. Add the potato slices to boiling water and boil them till tender but firm.

Do not over boil, as it will make the slices soft and break. Drain the potatoes and keep aside.

3 Blend yogurt and 1 tsp cornstarch in a small mixer till smooth. Keep aside.

4 Heat a pan on low heat. Add garlic. Stir for a few seconds. Add 1 tbsp flour. Stir till light brown. Add the milk, stirring continuously till slightly thick.

5 Reduce heat. Add the chopped dill, chillies, salt, pepper and the boiled potato slices.

6 Add the yogurt mixture. Stir for a minute to coat the potatoes nicely in sauce.

7 Reduce heat. Add a few drops of lemon juice if you like. Remove from heat. Serve hot with garlic bread.

Broccoli Stir fry

A wonderful gourmet dish combining broccoli with onions and tomatoes with just the right spices.

Serves 4

INGREDIENTS

250 g/8 oz broccoli - cut into medium
sized florets (2 cups florets)
1 tsp cumin seeds (*jeera*)
2 onions - cut into rings (1 cup)
a thin slice of ginger - cut into match
sticks (1 tbsp)
2 fresh red or green chillies - deseeded
& cut into long pieces
2 tomatoes - chopped finely (1 cup)
1½ tbsp tomato ketchup
2 tsp curry powder
½ tsp paprika
1 tsp salt
¼ cup milk

METHOD

1 Heat a non stick pan/skillet. Reduce heat. Add cumin. Wait till golden.

2 Add onion, ginger and green chillies. Cook till onions start turning brown.

3 Add curry powder and salt. Mix for a few seconds.

4 Add tomatoes and ketchup. Stir fry for 3-4 minutes.

5 Add broccoli. Stir fry for 2-3 minutes without covering. Cover and cook on low heat for 8-10 minutes or till done.

6 Add paprika. Stir fry without covering for 2-3 minutes.

7 Remove from heat. Add milk and mix well. Serve hot.

Ratatouille

A sunny Mediterranean speciality – vegetables and lots of tomatoes with basil.

Serves 4

INGREDIENTS

2 long, thin brinjals - cut into ¼" thick slices
2 zucchinis or *tori* - cut into ¼" thick slices
1 large red bell pepper - cut into ½" squares
1 onion - cut into slices
3-4 flakes garlic - crushed (½ tsp)
¼ tsp pepper - freshly ground
¼ tsp sugar, salt to taste
1 tsp dry basil
2 tbsp chopped fresh basil
2 tomatoes - roughly chopped into ½" pieces

METHOD

1 Place the eggplants in a colander. Sprinkle salt and let sit for 30 minutes. Rinse thoroughly. Drain and pat the eggplants dry on a clean kitchen towel.

2 Heat a non stick pan/skillet, add onion and garlic and stir for a few seconds till onion turns soft.

3 Add brinjals and zucchini. Saute for 3-4 minutes. Cover and cook on low heat for 8-10 minutes till brinjals are done.

4 Add red pepper and tomatoes and cook for 2-3 minutes without covering. Do not overcook.

5 Add salt, pepper, sugar, dry and fresh basil. Stir fry for a minute. Serve hot.

CHICKEN

Lemon Chicken

An appetising combination of chicken and bell pepper with a refreshing lemon tang – a clean and healthy taste.

Serves 4

INGREDIENTS

750 g/1½ lb chicken with bones - cut
Into 8 pieces or 400 g/12 oz boneless
chicken - cut into 1½-2" pieces
½ tsp pepper, salt, or to taste
3 tbsp lemon juice
3 cups ready-made chicken stock
2 bell peppers - cut into 2" cubes (you
can use 1 red and 1 green)
1 tbsp Worcestershire sauce
3 tbsp cornstarch dissolved in ½ cup
water

GARNISH
rind of 1 lemon
8-10 blanched almonds

METHOD

1 Marinate the chicken pieces with ½ tsp salt, ½ tsp pepper and lemon juice for 15 minutes.

2 Heat a pan, add the chicken. Stir fry for 3-4 minutes on medium heat.

3 Add the stock. Cook covered for about 15 minutes or till the chicken turns tender.

4 Add the bell peppers and Worcestershire sauce. Bring to a boil.

5 Mix cornstarch with ½ cup of water add to the chicken mixture. Cook stirring till thick. Check seasoning and add more salt & pepper if necessary. Remove from heat.

6 Serve garnished with lemon rind and blanched almonds.

Note: *In the absence of stock, use 3 cups water mixed with 2 soup/stock cubes.*

Chicken Stew

Nourishing comfort food at its best – chicken & vegetables stewed with aromatic spices.

Serves 4

INGREDIENTS

400 g/12 oz boneless chicken - cut into
2" pieces
1 bay leaf (*tej patta*)
2-3 cloves (*laung*)
3-4 peppercorns (*saboot kali mirch*)
2½ cups ready-made chicken stock
or
2 soup/stock cubes mixed with
2½ cups water

SAUCE
1½ cups milk, approx.
3 tbsp flour (*maida*)
½ carrot - cut into ½" cubes
4 green beans - cut into 2" pieces
¼ cup shelled peas
salt to taste, ½ tsp white pepper
some chopped parsley

METHOD

1 Heat a non stick pan/skillet. Add bay leaf, peppercorns and cloves. Dry roast for a few seconds.

2 Add the chicken pieces. Stir fry for 1-2 minutes.

3 Add stock. Cook on low heat for 15 minutes or till chicken is tender. Remove from heat.

4 Remove the chicken pieces and strain the stock. Reserve the chicken stock, discard the bay leaf, peppercorns and cloves.

5 For the sauce, mix enough milk, about 1½ cups with the chicken stock to get 4 cups of liquid. Keep aside.

6 Heat a pan. Add flour and stir till light brown. Reduce heat. Add the milk-stock mixture and stirring continuously, bring to a boil.

7 Add the vegetables (carrots, green beans and peas) and cook on low heat for 2-3 minutes.

8 Add the chicken pieces and pepper/salt if needed. Add chopped parsley and cook till you get the desired consistency.

9 Remove from heat. Serve hot with slices of bread, grilled till crisp.

Baked Chicken with Spinach

This can be the best baked dish you have presented at a party – a layer of spinach with garlic, then a layer of chicken with corn, covered with a golden topping.

Serves 6-7

INGREDIENTS

500 g/1 lb chicken with bones
1 onion - chopped fine (½ cup)
4 medium tomatoes - ground to a puree
½ cup ready-made tomato puree
1¼ tsp salt, ½ tsp pepper
¼ cup corn
1 tsp red chilli powder

SPINACH LAYER
6 cups finely chopped spinach - washed
& strained well to remove all water (press
spinach in the strainer to drain well)
1 tsp garlic paste or finely chopped
¾ tsp salt, ¾ tsp pepper, or to taste
2 tbsp tomato ketchup
2 tbsp yogurt

TOPPING
some dry bread crumbs
1 tomato - cut into thin wedges

METHOD

1 Boil or steam chicken. Cool and shred into small pieces.

2 In a non stick pan/skillet, add chopped onion, pureed tomatoes, tomato puree. Give 2-3 boils.

3 Add shredded chicken. Add salt pepper and red chilli powder to taste. Mix well. Give a few boils and cook till nearly dry. Add corn. Mix. Remove chicken from pan.

4 Put spinach in the pan. Add garlic, ¾ tsp salt and ¾ tsp pepper. Cook on high heat till spinach is reduced and all the water has evaporated. The spinach should be dry. Add tomato ketchup and yogurt. Mix well.

5 Take a baking dish. Spread spinach at the bottom.

6 Spread the prepared chicken on top of the spinach to form a layer.

7 Sprinkle bread crumbs on top of the chicken to cover.

8 Decorate with sliced tomato wedges and bake in a preheated oven at 150°C/300°F for 15 minutes.

Note: *Instead of chicken, fish can also be used.*

Chicken Grilled with Orange Juice

Five-star elegance – chicken is soaked in an orange marinade then grilled; the marinade is reduced, then poured on top – delightful!

Serves 2

2 Mix all ingredients except cornstarch. Marinate chicken for 6-8 hours turning over chicken pieces 2-3 times.

3 Heat a grill pan. Remove chicken pieces from marinade. Sprinkle some more pepper on top and grill for 10-12 minutes or till chicken is well cooked and crisp. Baste in between with the marinade to prevent the chicken from turning dry. Alternately cook in the oven for 15-20 minutes or on a greased non stick pan. In the pan, cover the chicken and after it is cooked increase heat to dry all water and cook it crisp.

4 Place chicken pieces on a serving dish.

5 Mix cornstarch to the remaining marinade.

6 Give 1-2 boils. Pour over the prepared chicken & serve hot along with some steamed vegetables.

INGREDIENTS

300 g/10 oz chicken (1 leg & 1 breast piece)
3 tbsp lemon juice
½ cup fresh orange juice
4-6 cloves garlic - chopped fine or minced (1 tsp)
1 tsp tabasco or chilli sauce
1 tbsp chopped fresh coriander/cilantro
1 tsp salt
¾ tsp coarsely ground peppercorns
1 tsp cornstarch

METHOD

1 Wash and pat dry the chicken pieces on a kitchen towel. Make 2 incisions on each piece.

FISH

Fish Creole

Fish is steamed in spiced tomato gravy to absorb the exotic flavours. Prawns/shrimps can be cooked in the same way. Serve with coriander rice.

Serves 3-4

INGREDIENTS

300 g/10 oz fish - cut into 2" pieces, preferably fillet & boneless, however other fish can also be used
2 tbsp lemon juice to wash fish
1 medium onion - chopped finely
1 large bell pepper - chopped finely
¾ cup tomato puree
1 tsp dry basil
5 tbsp chilli sauce
1 tbsp vinegar
1 tsp salt, or to taste, 1 tsp sugar
2 tsp cornstarch dissolved in ¼ cup water

TO SERVE

¾ cup chopped coriander/cilantro
3-4 cups boiled rice

METHOD

1 Rub the fish with some lemon juice to remove the fishy odour. Wash and pat dry on a kitchen towel or with a tissue napkin.

2 Heat a non stick pan/skillet. Add onion and bell pepper. Saute for 2 minutes on low heat.

3 Add tomato puree, basil, chilli sauce, vinegar, salt and sugar. Stir for 1-2 minutes.

4 Add ½ cup water. Give one boil.

5 Add fish in a single layer.

6 Cook uncovered for 6-7 minutes. (Turn over fish after 3-4 minutes) or till fish is thoroughly cooked.

7 Remove fish pieces with a slotted spoon on to a serving dish.

8 To the gravy in the nonstick pan, add cornstarch dissolved in ¼ cup of water.

9 Give one boil. Cook for a minute on low heat. Pour over fish.

10 Serve with boiled rice to which a lot of coriander is added at the time of serving and mixed well.

Oven Fried Fish

The fish looks and tastes fried but in fact it is baked! Low cholesterol and zero oil – a must-try recipe.

Serves 4-5

INGREDIENTS

500 g/8 oz fish, preferably fillet - cut into
2" pieces to get 8-9 pieces
¾ cup bread crumbs
1 tsp salt (adjust to taste)
1 tsp pepper (adjust to taste)
1 tsp lemon juice
1 egg white, ¼ tsp salt and ¼ tsp pepper
1 tbsp milk

METHOD

1 Wash and dry fish on paper towels.

2 Sprinkle salt, pepper and lemon juice on fish and mix well. Leave for 15 minutes.

3 Beat egg white lightly with ¼ tsp each of salt and pepper.

4 Dip fish pieces one by one in egg white and coat well with bread crumbs spread out in a plate.

5 Line a baking tray with foil and grease it lightly with milk. Place fish on it and bake in a preheated oven at 230°C/450°F for 10 minutes.

Note: *Time of baking will depend on the thickness of the fish. Chicken can also be made in the same way.*

Lemon Fish Florentine

Fillets of Sole fish are topped with low fat cheese sauce and baked on a bed of spinach.

Serves 4

INGREDIENTS

8 boneless fish fillets
1 tbsp lemon juice
½ tsp each of salt and pepper
500 g/1 lb spinach
¼ tsp nutmeg, ¼ tsp sugar, ¼ tsp salt
½ cup low fat cheese grated

SAUCE
3 tbsp plain flour (*maida*)
2 cups (450 ml/15 oz) milk
½ tsp salt
½ tsp peppercorns - coarsely crushed

METHOD

1 Remove the stem of the spinach leaves and shred the leaves. Wash well and strain. Squeeze the excess water. Keep aside in the strainer.

2 Wash and pat dry the fish fillet on a paper towel and marinate with lemon juice, salt and pepper. Keep aside for ½ hour.

3 Grease a non stick pan/skillet with ½ tsp oil or non stick cooking spray. Keep on heat and add the fish fillet. Cook fish on both sides on medium heat, till light brown and cooked. Drain and keep aside. Remove from pan.

4 In the same pan, add shredded spinach and cook till all the water evaporates. Add nutmeg, sugar and salt to taste. Keep spinach aside.

5 To prepare the sauce, whisk all ingredients of the sauce together. Cook on medium heat, stirring continuously, till the sauce thickens. Add salt & pepper to taste.

6 Stir half of the sauce into the cooked spinach mixture and spread the spinach in white sauce in a shallow oven proof dish.

7 Arrange the cooked fish pieces over the spinach.

8 Pour the remaining sauce over the fish & top with grated low fat cheese.

9 Bake in a preheated oven at 200°C/ 400°F for 15-20 minutes or till cheese melts. Serve hot with garlic bread.

Fish Kebobs

The marinade is a lemon-mint chutney – these out-of-this-world melting morsels of fish are lightly baked.

Serves 2-3

INGREDIENTS

350 g/12 oz fish - cut into 2" pieces
1 tsp oregano
1½ tbsp green mint paste or mint chutney
½ tsp black peppercorns - crushed
3 tbsp lemon juice
2 tbsp Worcestershire sauce
¾ tsp salt, or to taste
1 tsp minced garlic

METHOD

1 Prick each fish piece with a fork so that the marinade can penetrate well.

2 Mix everything together and let the fish marinate in it for 3-4 hours in the refrigerator.

3 Skewer the pieces of fish on bamboo or metal skewers. Line a tray with aluminium foil and spray it with a non stick spray. Place fish on it and bake in a hot oven at 230°C/450°F for 25-30 minutes. Serve with onion rings sprinkled with lemon juice.

Note: *The fish used should preferably be without skin and non-oily.*

DESSERTS

Hawaiian Pineapple with Rum Sauce

Pineapple, rum and brown sugar create the right island-holiday mood – rum sauce is the extra bonus!

Serves 6

INGREDIENTS

1 ripe pineapple
2-3 tbsp brown or white sugar
3 tbsp rum

SAUCE
2 cups milk
2 tbsp sugar
1 tbsp rum
2 tbsp custard powder
1 tbsp cocoa
4-5 almonds - slivered and toasted

METHOD

1 Remove the hard skin of the pineapple and remove the eyes. Cut the pineapple into ½" thick round slices and remove the center hard core to get rings.

2 Place the pineapple rings in a plate. Pour 3 tbsp rum and sprinkle 2-3 tbsp sugar over the pineapple slices and keep aside for ½ hour.

3 Heat a non stick pan add the pineapple rings and cook on medium heat till dry and sugar coats the slices.

4 Arrange the pineapples in a serving dish, overlapping the rings slightly.

5 For the sauce, dissolve custard and cocoa in ½ cup milk.

6 Heat the remaining 1½ cups milk with sugar in a heavy bottomed deep pan. Bring to a boil. Add the dissolved custard & cocoa to the boiling milk, stirring continuously. Cook for 5 minutes till it thickens to a thick pouring custard. Remove from heat. Taste sugar.

7 Add 1 tbsp of rum to the custard sauce. Pour the sauce over the pineapples. Sprinkle crushed toasted almonds and serve cold.

Note: *To toast almonds, sliver them into thin long pieces. Place in a microwave in a single layer for 3-4 minutes. Let them cool & use.*

Pina Cheesecake

A marvellous cheesecake made from paneer, hung yogurt and gelatine – and pineapple all the way.

Serves 12

INGREDIENTS

BASE
25 digestive biscuits, 8 tbsp milk, approx.

CHEESE CAKE FILLING
1 litre/1¾ pints (skimmed milk) + 2 tbsp
vinegar or 1 tsp citric acid crystals
2-3 tbsp cheese spread (plain)
2 cups yogurt - hang for 30 minutes
1 tin pineapple slices
1½ cups pineapple syrup from the tin
4 tsp gelatine
12 tablets artificial sweetener or
6 tbsp powdered sugar
2 egg whites
4 slices pineapple - chopped very finely
½ tsp pineapple essence
few drops yellow colour
1 tbsp lemon juice

TOPPING
1 tsp cornstarch & 1 tsp sugar dissolved
in ½ cup milk
½ tsp pineapple or lemon essence
few drops green colour
a lemon twist
2 pineapple slices - cut into very thin
slices

METHOD

1 Crush biscuits roughly in a small mixer grinder. Remove from grinder and add enough milk to bind the mixture. Spread the biscuits at the bottom of a loose bottom tin (7" -8" diameter) or a serving dish. Press. Place in the fridge to set.

2 Boil milk. Reduce heat. Add vinegar or citric acid, so as to curdle milk. Remove from heat and strain to get home made cheese/paneer.

3 Place hung curd (measure to 1 cup), paneer and cheese spread in a blender and blend to a smooth paste. Remove to a bowl.

4 Sprinkle gelatine on 1½ cups syrup. Soak for 2-3 minutes. Cook on low heat till gelatine dissolves. Remove from heat.

5 Add sugar or artificial sweetener to gelatine. Mix well to dissolve.

6 Mix 2-3 tbsp yogurt mix into the hot gelatine. Add the gelatine mix gradually into the remaining yogurt, stirring continuously with the other hand. Mix well. Add the essence, lemon juice, chopped pineapple and colour also to the cheese cake mixture. Mix well.

7 Beat the egg whites till stiff. Fold in stiff egg whites gently. Pour over the biscuit base. Keep in the fridge to set.

8 For the topping, mix cornstarch and sugar in milk & keep on heat. Bring to a boil, stirring continuously, till a thick sauce is ready. Remove from heat and let it cool down. Add colour and essence.

9 Pour on the set cheese cake with a spoon. Brown pineapple rings in a pan, turning sides. Cut it from any one end roll gently to make cones. Arrange a bunch on the cheesecake. Serve cold.

Devil's Chocolate Mousse

This sophisticated chocolate dessert has no cream at all – sweetened whipped yogurt is equally effective.

Serves 4

INGREDIENTS

2½ cups milk
2 tbsp cornstarch
3 tbsp cocoa
18 tablets of artificial sweetener
2½ tsp gelatine
2 cups yogurt - hang for ½ hour in a cheese cloth and squeeze well to remove all whey
1½ tsp vanilla essence

GARNISH

whipped hung sweetened yogurt
glace cherries, chocolate thins

METHOD

1 Dissolve cornstarch in ½ cup warm milk.

2 Put cocoa in a heavy bottomed pan. Pour ½ cup water on it and mix well. Keep on heat and stir continuously on low heat, for about 2 minutes till a dark paste is ready. Remove from heat.

3 Add the rest of the milk to cocoa paste and mix well using a wire whisk. Mix the cocoa on the sides of the pan nicely with the milk.

4 Keep on heat. When it starts boiling, add the dissolved cornstarch paste, stirring continuously. Cook, stirring till the milk turns slightly thick, like custard and coats the spoon. Remove from heat

5 Mix in artificial sweetener. Keep chocolate custard aside.

6 Sprinkle gelatine on ¼ cup water kept in a small pan. Stir on low heat till gelatine dissolves. Remove from heat and add hot gelatine to the chocolate custard. Let it cool down.

7 Whip the hung yogurt with a whisk till smooth. Add essence also.

8 Keeping 2 tbsp aside for topping, add the remaining yogurt mix to the cooled chocolate custard and mix well.

9 Check sugar. Add 1-2 tbsp powdered sugar if required, depending on the sourness of the yogurt.

10 Transfer to individual serving cups or a dish and keep in the fridge for 3-4 hours or till set. Garnish with whipped yogurt, thins and cherries.

GLOSSARY OF NAMES/TERMS

Al dente
Noodles and vegetables should be cooked to a texture that is not too soft; it should be 'firm to bite' which in Italian is 'al dente'.

Basil
A fragrant herb

Baste
To brush food with fat to prevent it from drying out.

Bean Curd
See tofu

Blanch
To remove skin by dipping into hot water for a couple of minutes. e.g. to blanch tomatoes or almonds.

Black salt
Kala namak

Blend
To combine two or more ingredients.

Bell Pepper
Capsicum

Cilantro
See coriander

Coriander, fresh
A green herb. All parts of the plant are flavourful and hence edible - leaves, stalks and the Thai also use the root of coriander. Also called cilantro in the west.

Cornflour
Cornstarch

Chickpeas
Garbanzo beans

Chutney, (mango)
Condiment of fruit, vinegar and spices

Dice
To cut into small neat cubes.

Dough
A mixture of flour, liquid etc., kneaded together into a stiff paste or roll.

Drain
To remove liquid from food.

Eggplant
Brinjal, baingan

Fish Sauce
A fermented sauce prepared from small fish

Garnish
To decorate.

Green Onion
Spring onions, scallions

Galangal
Thai ginger

Green Beans
Also called French beans. The tender variety should be used.

Juliennes
To cut into thin long pieces, like match sticks.

Kaffir Lime
A variety of lime found in Thailand

Lemon Grass
Imparts a lemony flavour to the food

Marinate
To soak food in a mixture for some time so that the flavour of the mixture penetrates into the food.

Paneer
The Indian cheese prepared from milk.

Plain Flour
All purpose flour, *maida*.

Red Chilli Powder
Cayenne pepper

Rind
The outer skin of citrous fruits like lemon, orange etc.

Saute
To toss and make light brown in shallow fat.

Shred
To cut into thin, long pieces.

Sift
To pass dry ingredients through a fine sieve.

Snow Peas
The whole flat green pods are edible; the peas are not fully formed.

Star Anise
A star-shaped, fennel-flavoured fruit, dried and used as a spice.

Tofu
Cheese prepared from soya bean milk. Also called bean curd.

Turmeric
A yellow spice with antiseptic properties. Usually available as a powder. It imparts a yellow colour to food.

Toss
To lightly mix ingredients without mashing them e.g. salads.

Zucchini
Tori